All I Learned At Boarding School Is That Knife Begins With An 'S'

This book is produced by KME.

Copyright © Daly Kelly 2026

The moral right of the author has been asserted in accordance with the Copyright Amendment (Moral Rights) Act 2000.

All rights reserved. Except as permitted under the Australian Copyright Act 1968 (for example, fair dealing for the purposes of study, research, criticism or review) no part of this publication may be reproduced, stored in a retrieval system, or transmitted in any form or by any means, electronic, mechanical, photocopying, recording or otherwise, without the written permission of the publisher.

Title:	All I Learned At Boarding School Is That Knife Begins With An 'S'
Author:	Kelly, Daly
ISBN:	978-0-646-73311-1
Subjects:	BIOGRAPHY & AUTOBIOGRAPHY / Memoirs

Cover design by Daly Kelly.

All I Learned At Boarding School Is That Knife Begins With An 'S'

Daly Kelly

Contents

Introduction/Foreword/Prologue/Preface............................7
Orientation..9
Jail versus Haven...14
Year Eight..16
Food & the Dining Room..18
Six Fish...22
Saturday Work..24
Year Nine...27
Oxen...29
Mabé (pronounced 'mar-bear')..32
Six-Hour Detentions..33
Year Ten...36
New Kids...39
Gym Dances..41
Hot Teachers...43
Rugby...45
Touch..47
The Infirmary...51
Year Eleven...55
Pornography...57
The Birth of MSN..59
Theft...60
Fight Club..63
Physics – No Worries..68
Tunnelling..71
Year Twelve...75
Lingo...77
Margaret Keetles..78
Mr Jones..80
Year Eight Punishment...83

Keith	85
The Formal	88
Graduation	91
Schoolies	95
Pregnancy – What the...?	98
About the Author	101
Appendices	102

Introduction/Prologue/Foreword/Preamble/Preface

The purpose for writing this book is simple: it was written to entertain. This book was not designed as a precursor to boarding school. In fact, the author would like to warn those who are about to attend boarding school for the first time to seriously consider closing this book and never re-opening it. For the events described in this book are not completely accurate, nor are they what the average person would expect, coming from a boarding school.

That being said, it is by no means my intention for people to read this book as a fictional novel. For although I have taken a certain amount of poetic license in writing this book, that should in no way detract from the credibility of the stories I will share. After reading this, I hope you feel compelled to read on...

My name is Daly Kelly, and I attended boarding school from the 27th of January 2000 to the 17th of November 2004. In this time, I shared many experiences with my peers, and I felt that many of these were worthy of publication. And so here comes the story of my life at boarding school!

(With several additions, deletions, and omissions.)

Orientation

Everyone remembers their first day of school, don't they? In this same way, I can guarantee you that everyone remembers their whole first week at boarding school.

To get to Brisbane from Rockhampton was quite an adventure for a youthful (and somewhat naïve) 12-year-old. Originally, I had said most of my goodbyes at the Rockhampton train station. There was my older sister (Danyelle – 14), my younger half-sister (Korrina – 3), and my stepfather (Shane), all of whom I wouldn't see for another ten weeks.

Everyone who has ever spent a great deal of time away from loved ones at such a young age knows how hard it is to say goodbye, and I was no exception. There were tears, and there were 'I love you's, and all the nonsensical interactions that we share with family members before our long stays away from each other.

Once we arrived in Brisbane, I was introduced to public transport! Oh, what an adventure! The bus driver looked like he was ready to kick me off the bus when I held my money out for him, instead of putting it on his little tray! Anyway, we stayed for a few days with friends in Brisbane before we arrived at what was to be my main place of residence, and census address, for the next five years.

As I walked into the year eight dorm for the first time, lugging a 30kg+ suitcase (I knew it was over 30 kilos because the bag Nazis at the train station hadn't allowed us to check the luggage), I couldn't help but marvel at some of the boys' names which were posted above their beds. Two in particular are still stuck in my mind: Jimmy New and Justin Neilsen. Sadly, neither of them made it past year nine; however, I have never forgotten either of them – for the simple fact that their names were so ironical the first time I saw them. Here I was, a young kid, leaving my parents for the first time, and two of these boys' names fitted the script perfectly: Jimmy New, because he was new to the school like the rest of us, and Justin, because he was just in…

The first night my mother and I had planned well. I was to say goodbye to her, and then move promptly to have a shower. That way, if there were any tears to come, I wouldn't be an object of ridicule for all the other boys at school. However, this ideal parting wasn't meant to be, for my boarding supervisors had other plans. Soon after the parents had left, we (the students) all gathered as a group and headed up to the gym.

Saying that I came back to the dormitory tired would be an understatement – we were wrecked. That was the first time that I can remember staying up past ten o'clock on a school night.

The next morning was our year eight orientation day, the day when all the year eights learnt about high school. What a shock! I had no idea that a place could be this big! There were so many people, and we were only the year eights! Anyway, in general, the actual school part (this is most commonly referred to as the day-school) was alright, it was the boarding aspect that was going to take some getting used to; in particular, adopting the punctual nature which everyone else seemed to possess except for myself. There were roll-calls and meal times and afternoon check-offs and lots of hustle and bustle generally. As the saying goes, I didn't have time to scratch myself. So naturally, of those first weeks, I have very few memories indeed. That isn't to say that it was an easy task to settle into boarding school – it was in fact very difficult.

This is a warning for all those in the process of wrapping themselves up and posting themselves to the nearest boarding school: the place you're going to is not the same place that's in the glossy school magazines – there are no kids smiling and rolling in the grass. It is a completely different world. You won't really know until you get there, but the best thing to do is to prepare for the worst.

Over the next few weeks, I became accustomed to boarding school, but in no way did I start liking it. I got homesick – as everyone did. But it was an adventure, and I enjoyed the false sense of independence which boarding school offers young people. The supervisors seem to be able to make you feel like you can do whatever you like; whereas in truth, they are in complete control of you, and can rule you with an iron fist. However, I didn't particularly mind this aspect of boarding school at first – I was fairly happy being told what to do. Eventually though, this is one of the reasons why I was so joyous when my time at boarding school was over.

Many, many things struck me as odd or weird in my first weeks at school, and one of these was the way students addressed teachers. Arbitrarily, boys would call each of the male teachers 'sir,' and each of the female teachers 'miss' – save a few teachers, who insisted on being called by their full name. I was amazed by this: it was so impersonal, but at the same time, I felt lower-classed as I started calling these teachers by the same title that Donald Bradman had received from the Queen in recognition of his outstanding cricketing skills.

Nevertheless, I eventually got used to this system of naming, and saw its benefits. For instance, you never actually had to know a teacher's name; you could simply call them by their alias. It was like the way the characters in George Orwell's *1984* were required to call each other 'comrade.' It wasn't hard for the year eights to learn each of their teachers' names; meanwhile the teachers had a much harder job. Some of them had to learn in excess of 250 boys' names at the start of every year, not an easy task at all.

One of the things that used to annoy me the most about boarding school was its monotony. It was simply too repetitive: get up, get dressed, go to breakfast – have school all day, come back to the dorm – spend your afternoon doing whatever you like, then have a shower – go to dinner, go to study, go to bed. And then that whole thing again tomorrow. It almost makes boarding school seem like a jail…

Jail versus Haven

At times, boarding school is a real drag. You're always being told what to do, and you never get any privacy. However, at other times, boarding school was most definitely a blessing. It is the combination of these two feelings which makes boarding a unique lifestyle for teenagers.

The most notable event which makes boarding school seem like a jail (apart from its continuous monotony) was the nights during year nine, when Mr Mulheren was on duty. After we had finished quiet time, and it was time for lights out, he would walk out of the office and holler, 'LIGHTS OUT!' Every time he did this, it reminded me of the jailbreak movie cliché when the guard yells the same thing, right before the main actor escapes from the otherwise impenetrable fortress. This didn't particularly worry, me except that it made me think that here I was, being treated like I was in jail, but I was never going to escape like the heroes in the movies did.

On the other hand, boarding can be an escape. My relationship with my mother was certainly strengthened by the fact that we spent so much time apart from each other.

There were times when I was glad that she was at least six hundred kilometres away. Even worse still – and I hate to admit this – sometimes I was glad to be back at boarding school after the holidays. These particular times were when our family was having a hard time running a corner store, and everyone's patience was stretched to the limit.

Overall, I would like to express my deep gratitude toward boarding school for the values that it has taught me, in particular, equality. Without boarding school, there is no way that at such a young age, I would've come into contact with so many people from different backgrounds – and had to live with them. At least now, when I meet someone, I won't judge them at face value, but instead, I will try to get to know them first. This is because I can remember judging all the boys I schooled with when I first met them, and I realise now how much my opinion of them changed over the five years that I lived with them.

Year Eight

In year eight, our house parents were Mr and Mrs Corboy, recent ring-ins from some other boarding school up north. They were lovely people; however, after meeting, them my mother was of the strong opinion that Mr Corboy in particular was very shallow. I immediately adopted this opinion (as so often young people do), but I'm glad to say that my relationship with Mr Corboy didn't suffer because of this.

One of the most challenging and memorable things about being in year eight was wondering how to react to the requests of our house parents' daughters. It would have been alright if they'd been older, but they were only five and three years old!

They were obviously just copying their parents when they were telling us to take showers and collect our laundry, but after about the fifth time, even those with temperaments of steel began to falter. Eventually Mr and Mrs Corboy had stern words with their two girls, and after this, their telling us what to do was a very rare occasion indeed.

The year eight dorm was designed for extremely limited privacy and maximum control. This was achieved by the interior walls being built to ankle level, so that even an ant could've seen from one end of the dorm to the other. This annoyed us more and more every day, but eventually we all got over it. If there is one thing that I am completely immune to now, it's male nudity; it has no effect on me whatsoever. After five years of mooning, dacking, and nudie runs, it's difficult to make even the most conservative boarder blush.

Food and the Dining Room

The dining room at any boarding school is a sight to see, and MCA's dining room was no different. It was a rather large building, with another three smaller dining rooms attached. The large dining room was meant for the year eights, nines, tens and elevens, and the other three were reserved for the year twelves, the supervisors, and the brothers, respectively. Now that I come to think of it, the word 'dining' doesn't really describe the sort of mischief that went on in those rooms.

There were three meals served in the dining room each day: breakfast, lunch, and dinner. Breakfast was by far the best meal – the only one that was enjoyable. Lunch was usually a hamburger dripping with fat, or the like. And dinner – well, let's just say that dinner was well worth avoiding.

The serving structure changed whilst I was at school. Originally, the tables were set when we came in for a meal. However, once the senior tuckshop moved down to the dining room, everyone had to pick up their cutlery and crockery on their way to their seats. The end of the meal was always the same, though: scrape everything that you didn't eat into a receptacle/bin (which was usually most of the meal), put your plate on the trolley, your cup in a plastic container, and distribute your cutlery between the three marked containers: K, F, and S. It was at these containers that one of my most defining memories of boarding school was forged…

I had just finished about as much of my burnt-rare steak as I could handle, and was moving to dump it in the bin, along with my uneaten boiled vegetables and rock-hard potatoes. I had scraped my plate, stacked it, and was just about to separate my cutlery when I saw a big kid (probably a senior), come over and unload his eating utensils in about an eighth of the time that I was taking. In a moment, he was gone. He didn't even bother to separate his cutlery! Now this was an example I had to follow.

I did it slowly and cautiously the first time – checking to see if any supervisors were looking first – but after a few times, I realised that nobody actually cared whether or not you put your spoon in the fork container, or your fork in the knife container. Nobody cared that you didn't know what letter knife started with, and you 'accidentally' put it in the container with an 'S' on it. And so, I committed the first of my many misdeeds at boarding school.

Every meal at boarding school is a chore. No one actually wants to eat any of the food, but we are forced by the thought that we might otherwise die. This is why the school was able to serve such shocking food during the time that I was there:

they were working on one of the most basic human fears – the fear of starvation.

Now I don't say this willy-nilly, I have authority over this sort of subject. Marist College Ashgrove served shocking food in the time that I was there, and that's that. It doesn't mean that Marist is a bad school, nor does it mean that the other schools in Brisbane didn't serve equally bad food, it just means that MCA didn't (and probably doesn't) serve good food.

On the upside, the food at school did get mildly better while I was there. Slowly, some of the more hated meals were erased from the menu, and some better meals came in to replace them. But on the whole, the food tended to stay the same. For instance, we were served hotdogs about once a week, every week while I was at school. Then the kitchen decided they would change the brand of hotdog that they used. We absolutely hated the new hotdogs; they tasted like boiled vegetables. So they reverted to the original brand. About a year after this occurred, we managed to get hotdogs off the menu altogether, because they were hated so much. However, hotdogs returned to the menu some months later, only this time they had a new brand again. These hotdogs tasted mildly better than the originals, so we were mildly satisfied.

The most commonly eaten food that tasted good and was easiest to make at school was toast with butter cooked onto it. I've worked out that I probably consumed about 5000 pieces of this sort of toast in my time at MCA. The reason I ate it was because I enjoyed the taste, and also, it was too time consuming to make this sort of toast at home.

Six Fish

One of the few trends that ran all the way through to year twelve was 'six fish', and this was not without good reason. Farting, as everyone knows, is a very impolite act, especially when committed in public. Hence boarders have devised their own way of dealing with this bodily phenomenon, so that farting in a boarding school is a rare event indeed. The idea of this preventative technique revolves around the basic human fear of being punched. The concept is simple enough: fart, and you will be punched. This can occur in many different ways, a few of which are outlined below:

1. If you fart, and someone calls 'slug twenty,' then that person gets to punch you twenty times.

2. If you fart, and someone calls 'six fish,' then you have to name six different types of fish. While you are naming the fish, the person is allowed to punch you as many times as they like.

3. If you fart, and you're in the middle of a group of kids, and your fart is a particularly stinky fart, then you're going to be punched no matter what!

The first and second of these methods are far more interesting than the third, and thus the purpose of this chapter is to explain the significance of these two.

As to the origins of these amusements, I have absolutely no idea. Not only did six fish just seem to come out of the blue sometime in year eight, but it was born with such a passion that you had to hang onto something with two hands not to be dragged along with the group.

Naturally, nobody was exempt from the six fish rule. You couldn't simply say, "Oh, I don't play that game." Nor could you say, "If you punch me, then I'll punch you back." So eventually, everyone's natural instinct was to either fart when no one was around, or to simply hold it in.

Not long after this phenomenon hit boarding school, the 'safe' rule was invented. It allowed the perpetrator of the crime to call 'safe' after they fart, and that would disallow any other person from saying 'six fish' or 'slug twenty' et cetera. Nonetheless, the third rule from above ↑ still sometimes overrode this 'safe' rule.

Saturday Work

In many ways, the term 'character-building' can be considered an oxymoron. Character is something which is fairly concrete, and most would consider it unchangeable. However, there are still those few who use this term to coerce young boys into shovelling dirt and other such inane tasks. I am of course making a direct reference to our sessions with Brother Nick, the working bee fathers, and my fellow inmates.

Saturday work was a simple exercise. Once the rugby season had finished, we boarders were left at a loose end on Saturday mornings, so the school staff had us perform manual labour around the grounds. Most of the jobs that Br Nick had us complete were beneficial to the school, but from time to time, we would be forced to do things which seemed entirely pointless, and even looking back now, I can't see how moving dirt from one area to another, and then back again the next week helped the school. But I wasn't in charge of our character building, now, was I?

Now, only the year eights, nines and sometimes the year tens were required to do work, for the senior years were instead required to study on a Saturday morning. However, once I had made it to year twelve, Brother Nick and his faithful working bee fathers seemingly vanished. Well, they didn't so much vanish as fade away. There wasn't one particular Saturday morning that I noticed an absence of junior boys doing Saturday work. It just seemed like the work dried up. I suppose it was a bit like the industrial revolution; the jobs just seemed to disappear.

Now, this didn't worry me too much, until I left boarding school. Then I realised that among all of that whinging and griping during Saturday work, between the shouts of slavery and claims of workers compo, we boys really did enjoy and benefit from Saturday work. We made lifelong friends at boarding school, and we made them because we were forced to know each other as intimately as possible. And of course, this wouldn't have been possible without Saturday work. It was at Saturday work that you realised who the real workers were. You also learnt who the spectators were! It was at Saturday work that you could tell the difference between people willing to stick with a job, and those who will give up at the first hurdle. And Saturday work was where you realised who some of your best friends really were.

Now this may seem like a bit of a deep experience to have while doing odd jobs around a school, and to tell you the truth, reading over this, it does sound a bit airy-fairy. But you're just going to have to take my word for it – Saturday work was a life-changing experience for us boarders. And if you still don't get it, just put it down as one of those 'you had to be there' things.

Year Nine

Year nine seemed to be over in a flash. I had trouble extracting from my mind what particular events occurred within this marvellous time slot. However, I eventually came up with a few stories, which I hope you will enjoy.

In year nine, we had Mr Shayne Moniz as our boarding supervisor. Like all teachers, Mr Moniz had his own scrupulous way of running his classroom. However, none of us had yet realised how he ran a dormitory. To our shock and horror, it was precisely the same way that he ran his classroom – with absolute power.

Now, Mr Moniz was a forceful dorm-master. He didn't shout very often, nor did he ever get violent; however, he could exert his will upon you through detentions. The sheer weight and number of them could force even the most rebellious of us to change our ways. It was the combination of Moniz and Newman that made our lives sometimes feel like one big, never-ending detention.

You see, Mr Moniz and Mr Newman were the crime-fighting pair. If Moniz was Batman, then Newman was

Robin; if Moniz was the Phantom, then Newman was Hero; if Moniz was Frodo, then Newman was Sam; if Moniz was Ren, then Newman was…well, I'm sure you get my point by now.

It worked like this: if Mr Newman saw you doing something that he considered inappropriate, he would mark you down for a recommended detention. What a croc! A recommended detention wasn't even comparable to a slap on the wrist; it just gave us an excuse to hate Mr Newman. You see, very few of his recommended detentions ever made it past the recommendation stage. And if they did, they were either cut down severely or converted into a stern word or two from Mr Moniz. However, every once in a while, when Moniz had had a gutful, he would end up giving everyone all of their recommended detentions at once!

Oxen

'Oxen' is, without a doubt, one of the most fun games ever thought up. Or at least, that was what I thought in the latter part of year nine. The game is simple enough: all you need is an even number of people (four or six), a deck of cards (of the cheaper kind), a sturdy set of chairs, and a table.

To begin with, someone is nominated as the dealer (the dealer can play and deal at the same time). Everyone is dealt four cards and immediately inspects them. Once a few moments have passed, the dealer takes four cards from the deck and flips them right-side-up in the middle of the table. The idea of the game is to get four of a kind in your hand, so naturally, people start grabbing at the cards. However, you can only have four cards in your hand at once, so if you pick up three, then you must immediately put down three (etc). Once everyone has finished swapping cards with the ones that are on the table, the dealer asks the other players whether they would like to scrap the remaining cards, to which the players reply 'yes,' 'no,' or 'wait.' Once the cards have been scrapped, they take no further part in the game. Then the dealer takes four new cards from the deck and places them right-side-up in the centre of the table once again. The game can continue like this for some time.

When one finds themselves in the enviable position of having four of a kind, they are immediately subject to another problem – that of signalling their partner. You see, you don't simply win by having four of a kind: you must make some subtle signal to your partner, so that he can then say 'OXEN ON JIMMY,' for example. The signals can range from touching certain areas of the face to bursting into a set of fake hiccups. In general, the signals are kept non-vocal for the sake of fair play. The reason you must signal to your partner is because if the opposition (anyone in a pair other than your own) suspects that you have four-of-a-kind, then they can call Oxen on you, and then they win.

It was a combination of Oxen and farting which led to Kinsella's first beating…

However much we played it, we couldn't get enough. Oxen was all the rage. There were six of us one night, Brad and Kinsella, Matt McClelland and Eric, and the final pair was Webby and me. We were laughing and enjoying ourselves as we got deeper into the game. I don't know about other people, but a combination of laughing and movement tends to bring the methane within a boarder's body to the explosion point, and in one fit of laughter, Kinsella did just that: he farted.

Now, normally this would be all right; however, under certain circumstances, farting can put the whole dorm against you. Immediately after the fart, Matt called six fish; Kinsella was already making a break for it as the rest of us called either six fish or slug twenty. He'd committed a crime punishable by only one sentence: he had forgotten to say 'safe,' and now he was gonna pay.

There was no supervisor present, so as Matt started hitting Kinsella, we all joined in. In a few moments, Kinsella was on the ground, and the beating didn't stop there. Kinsella continued to squirm, until we decided that he'd had enough, and then we all joked about it. So the moral of the story is, don't fart; and if you're going to fart, make sure that you're ready to either take a beating or say 'safe.'

Mabé (pronounced 'mar-bear')

Oh, what an interesting chapter title, I bet it has your cogs turning! Now what's the best way to describe this wonderful character? Mabé was a person who was always full of energy. His real name was Richard Frazer, and he came from somewhere up north. The reason he was called Mabé was simple enough: he had a weird walking style, and this was viewed as a serious character flaw by many of us who were too young and too stupid to know any better, so we decided to give him a nickname reflecting his strange attribute. Apparently (and I am no expert when it comes to this) in pidgin, Mabé means 'he who walks crooked,' so this was a very fitting name for him.

Six-Hour Detentions

This was one of the most lethal punishments that could be given at boarding school (many of the other punishments are far too horrific and gruesome in nature to ever be mentioned, let alone written down!) It consisted of sitting in a classroom for six hours, doing the most mind-numbing tasks, on a Sunday, while everyone else was allowed to do as they please. I was lucky, in that I only ever received one six-hour detention...

It was an ordinary Friday night at boarding school. We had been playing Oxen in the middle dorm all afternoon. We continued oxen at every interval we could for the rest of the night, and only realised when quiet time was called that we hadn't yet showered. Webb and I decided to wait until everyone was in bed (and hopefully asleep), before we got up (a heinous crime in itself) and made our way quietly to the shower room. We showered quickly and returned to our rooms. But this was enough to trigger a night of fun.

We had roused the more daring members of our dorm in the process of showering, and while we were gone, a pillow fight had begun. We suppressed school-girl giggles as we raced around the dorm, hitting each other over the head with the pillows. It was fun because we knew we weren't allowed to do it! However our fun was to be short-lived.

To put it bluntly, we were busted. Mr Dieckman, the supervisor on night duty, rose from his obviously very light slumber, and made his way sneakily up the corridor, and turned on his torch just metres in front of us. I was lucky, in that there were a few people between me and him, so he probably didn't recognise me immediately. Webb and I acted quickly. We turned, and in the same movement launched ourselves toward our beds. We both made it to our beds, while the other offenders were escorted to the office. As I lay under my doona, trying to remain inconspicuous, I thought to myself, "I'm going to be ferreted out, it's only a matter of time." But I was happy there, waiting to be caught.

Mr Dieckman shone the torch up and down me once, before the circular pool of light came to rest on where my head would be (i.e. if my doona wasn't covering it!) The light remained there for what seemed like an eternity while Mr Dieckman judged me guilty or innocent.

"Get up, and wait outside the office, Daly," Mr Dieckman said very calmly. I did just as he said.

Outside the office, the atmosphere was electric! We all knew we'd been caught, and there was no way out of it now, but the question running through all of our minds was whether or not we would nark on those who were involved, but hadn't been caught by Mr Dieckman. To our credit, I don't think anyone else got into trouble except for those present outside the office.

The condemnation was swift. We were all to be present in nine days time for a six-hour detention.

The detention was almost unbearable. More mind-numbing than writing out lines, worse than copying out of the dictionary – this detention was the worst detention that I have ever had to endure. It's amazing how long six hours seems when you're drawing a tree which represents your family, or reflecting on why little Jimmy stole the cookie. The tasks that they had allotted for us to complete were utterly puerile. They were punishing us the way you punish a six-year-old, not the way you punish a twelve-year-old. However, we managed to make our way through the ordeal, and have lived to tell the tale.

Year Ten

Mr Baldwin, what can I say? He is probably one of the nicest men that I have met in my life. He is a large man with a John Travolta smile, and an unlimited supply of one-liners. Without Mr Baldwin, the boarding section of Marist College Ashgrove, and ultimately the rest of the school, would have had a lot of trouble operating.

On the very first night of year ten, about twenty-five minutes after lights out, the year got under way…

I first heard a few boys whispering, and then someone ran down the hall. I knew that Mr Baldwin would not be in the mood for any trouble this early in the term, so I stayed in bed. As I predicted, about a minute later, the lights were flicked on, and a bellowing voice commanded us to the common room. Once there, I knew immediately that I would be scrutinized. For although I wasn't involved in any way, shape or form, the people that were *involved were caught red-handed at the end of my bed.*

Everyone who was awake moved directly to the common room. There was grumbling from the sleepy, and nervous chatter from the guilty. I was somewhere in between, for although I was not involved, I wasn't very tired, and I probably looked more awake than I should've. Mr Baldwin scrutinized everybody for a few minutes, before giving us a spiel about how we shouldn't be at boarding school if we were going to involve ourselves in this sort of rot, and how we were wasting our parents' money, et cetera. I'd heard it all before, and wasn't in the mood to be told off on my first night back for something I hadn't even been involved in.

Mr Baldwin ended his talk only after he was thoroughly sure that no one had enjoyed their earlier fun as much as they had hated his speech. He then proceeded to return people to their beds, as if pronouncing 'you're innocent.' His finger swung over me, and he stated, "I don't know about you – yet."

To which I mumbled something incoherent, which probably pronounced my false guilt. I was boiling; I couldn't believe that Mr Baldwin of all people would think that I was involved. However, it took Mr Baldwin only a few short minutes to figure out the guilty parties, and the sentencing was even shorter. I was not present for the latter, as Mr Baldwin had kindly returned me to my bed – and my faith in him was restored.

With that, year ten had begun!

This was to be the middle of my boarding career. However, it was not one of the more enjoyable years. People were suspended, people were expelled, and people were threatened with butter knives. Ducks were caught and then released, crows were killed with pillows, and it was the first year that the dorm didn't gel together as a group. As you can see, year ten was a time for change.

New Kids

As soon as year ten began, I knew that it was going to be a different year. About a month in, I realised why.

Imagine having a well-working fish colony. You have about thirty fish, all of which are different sizes, and are comfortable with that. The fish are happy. Then all of a sudden, you throw in an assortment of other smaller fish, they all are timid for a while, and then suddenly, all of the smaller fish start biting each other, as well as the original fish. Some get bigger, and some get smaller, and some stay the same, but in general, there is chaos and confusion. After a while, the fish start to settle down, and once again you have equilibrium.

This is the best analogy for a boarding school. The smaller fish enter at the beginning of the year (mainly years ten and eleven), the size of the fish equals its reputation amongst dorm members, and the whole process takes about fifteen weeks! So as you can see, the beginning of each year is usually a very turbulent time at any boarding school, however this is especially true for years 10 and 11, and this is when I started to have my first real doubts about having ever come to boarding school.

There were times when I would've gladly hopped on the next bus, train or plane, and made my way home. Thankfully, these times were few and far between. Generally speaking, instead of true home sickness, you have what my uncle so eloquently described as 'a longing for kin.' A problem where you just want to be yourself around people who must accept you for who you are (i.e. your family), but instead you are stuck in a place where initially no one will accept you, and you have to work for every ounce of respect you get. I got tired of playing everybody's games at times, and just felt like telling them to stick it, and then going home. But overall, boarding school was a blessing in disguise, and I'm glad that I stuck it out.

Gym Dances

Most of us had been waiting two years for these lovelies, but some unlucky people had been waiting as long as five years. Gym dances were one of the highlights of the term for us boarders; they were among our very few encounters with the opposite sex, so we took full advantage of them.

The reason we had been waiting for so long was that only year tenners and older were allowed to attend these events. Naturally, we were stoked when we walked into the gym for our first dance. Forty sex-starved boarders in a sea of over four hundred girls, who wouldn't be! We danced the night away, and realised that, like a lot of other things at school, it didn't match up to our expectations. Sure, they had loud music, they had flashing lights and smoke machines, but you get over that in about eight seconds, and what do you do for the other twelve thousand five hundred and ninety-two seconds? Another thing that tended to bother the boarders especially was that it was compulsory for us to go, but they still made us pay a ten dollar admission fee. We figured that if we were made to go, then they should at least waive the fee.

ALL I LEARNED AT BOARDING SCHOOL

The strangest thing that I ever noticed about gym dances was the shallowness of almost every person in the room. I couldn't tell you how many times I saw the same girl make out with three different guys in one night, and the same goes for guys.

Hot Teachers

While I was at MCA, more than half the teachers there were male. It was about a sixty-forty split. This, coupled with the fact that our school was single sex, made that forty percent the focus of much of our attention.

As my years at boarding school slowly passed, my standards fell slowly but surely. At school we had a system of rating chicks as to how attractive they were. The scale was from one to ten – however, most people neglected to even rate those below seven. I came to boarding school with standards of about a level seven. In about year ten I peaked, with standards at about a level eight. But from then on, it was all downhill. By the end of year twelve, my standards had fallen around my ankles, and I was down to about a level three.

Now, there were some teachers at school that were standouts in the field of looking good. I will call them Ms A, Ms B, and, the most attractive teacher I have ever met in my life, Ms C. I had a crush on this woman for the entire duration of my boarding life. I think that she probably found this out some time while I was in year ten. I was lucky enough to have her teach me for about two years of my time there, and those lessons were heaven. I mean, it's the little things that you learn to enjoy when you're a boarder, such as a smile from your favourite teacher, or just a hint of flirtatiousness when she returns your draft, telling you that it's a good piece of writing.

Some boys thought that my attitude toward her was unwarranted, even immoral, but I look at it this way: she was a beautiful woman, and I was a young and impressionable boy. Who can blame me for idolising her? On top of all this, she had a slight accent, and was one of the nicest teachers at MCA. The truth is that without her, my time at MCA would've been a lot less enjoyable – thank you Ms C.

Rugby

Marist College Ashgrove is most notable for its consistency in creating Wallaby-bound Rugby Union players. Since the inception of the College, it has schooled, if not created, no fewer than twenty-one international Rugby Union representatives. I know that I may be offending the Marist Brothers by saying this (and Catholics in general), but rugby is like a religion at Marist College Ashgrove.

The rugby craze first hit me in year eight, right between the eyes. As soon as rugby season started, there was a different aura about the school. Everyone seemed to want to get in on the action. Having never played before, I was interested in what these people were so fanatical about. I had played all of the other codes of football before (League, soccer, and AFL), but never before in my life had I seen such a change in the general atmosphere because of a sport. I just had to check it out.

The internal trials had begun, so I hurried to get my name down on the list entitled 'Those who have never played before'…

My first game of rugby was relatively blasé. I probably got the ball once or twice, probably got penalised once or twice, but in the end, I had a very fine time. I was vaguely beginning to understand why rugby could have such an effect on people.

In my first two years, I was merely a participant, not really a player. It was not until year ten that I started to *love* rugby. The sport grew on me. Every time rugby was mentioned, it was like someone was comforting me with a coat in the cold. I wondered why I felt this way, and it has taken me until now to realise why.

Rugby is the game that is said to be played in heaven. Of course, I don't think that anyone has any substantial evidence to support this absolutely outrageous claim; however, it is a nice thought. Rugby has somehow collected all of the best aspects of the football codes and combined them to create a variably moving, team-controlled, player-based masterpiece. The sport has one of the best balances between individual input and team contribution. Stars can shine in rugby, but at the same time, you cannot win with a team of champions. Other sports like touch or netball generally rely on the team to win games, and so does rugby – but unlike touch or netball, an individual in rugby can make a greater difference. Whereas in team sports like water polo and basketball, you can rely on a single player to win you the match – however, in rugby, you can't do this, or even allow yourself to think it.

Touch

At school, touch football was played even more than Rugby Union itself! Almost every afternoon in year nine, and nearly the same in year ten and eleven, was spent on the No. 2 (Derek Cameron) oval enjoying a good game of touch. It was so popular that at one time or another, there could be as many as four games of touch happening at once on the oval. Now if you've ever tried to fit four games of touch on one union field, it's a bit like fitting a lion, a crocodile, an elephant, and a great white in the same enclosure – everyone thinks they're top dog. The bickering was mainly instigated by the negotiation of boundaries of the different fields. Generally the older group of players would win the argument, but occasionally, a younger group with a lot more players would win through sheer weight of numbers.

The only thing that annoyed me about touch, and especially during my last two years, was the absence of any real structure to the game. There was, of course, never any referee present, and so a majority vote was usually the deciding decision. So, no one is surprised if someone runs in to score what they think is a legitimate try, but then the ball is brought back to a forward pass three plays ago.

General rules of boarders touch differ majorly from the accepted rules. These are a few examples:

- Must take at the beginning of the match, and after every try (one team kicks the ball to the other team, and they must catch it on the full)
- The ball was always allowed to hit the ground as long as it was knocked backward.
- A standard 0.2m defensive line is played.
- Kicks in general play are allowed.
- There is no half usually, and the person who is touched generally just taps the ball on their foot and offloads after they've been touched.

These rules made for a far more interesting game than just your standard touch game.

Touch was a very enjoyable game for all at boarding school, and it is something I will miss dearly. It might've been the fact that it was one of the few times that the boarders as a group got together to do something without the input of any other group at the college. It was something that we could call our own, something that we owned and loved. Playing touch gave boarders a sense of belonging.

Playing touch footy in the rain is probably the one thing that I have missed most about boarding school. Touch footy was always great fun, but when it started raining, the fun level increased exponentially. To tell you the truth, I don't really know why touch was so much better in the rain, but it just was.

The main difference between standard touch and touch-in-the-rain is that when it's raining, there are a lot more handling errors, and it's a lot harder to slow down. Ideally, there would be a few big collisions between players in any one match. These usually occurred between a decoy runner and someone in the defensive line, or when someone was about to score – and everyone starts running faster!

Another thing that was oh-so-enjoyable when we were playing touch in the rain was sliding in the puddles on the oval. Every time someone scored, we'd all get huge run-ups, and then launch ourselves into the miniature lakes that sprouted on the oval during a downpour. The distance you slid depended on what part of your body was touching the ground. If you slid on your gut, you usually got about five or six metres – and the same for your knees. However, if you slid on your backside (which we discovered was the best technique), you could slide upwards of ten metres. Of course, all this also depends on how fast you can run, and not surprisingly, some kids were better at it than others.

The truth is, when we played touch in the rain as a dorm, we were just a bunch of kids doing something fun and mischievous together. I can't tell you exactly why it was so fun. All I can tell you is that I am not alone in my fond memories of touch – there are many other old boys that share exactly the same view as me, that touch football is one of boarding school's defining qualities, and it is one of our fondest and most tangible memories of the place.

The Infirmary

'Infirmary' is quite a sesquipedalian word for a place where boarders went to bludge. An infirmary is defined in most dictionaries as a place where the sick or weak are cared for, but our infirmary played host to a great many other things. It was a place where you could wag school quite lawfully, it was a place where you could perve on whatever nurse was on duty, it was one of the few places in the school where you could get cold water, and finally – and this is only if you are either really bored, or really craving a soft drink – it was a place where you could attempt to steal a lemonade out of the fridge. No, this place shouldn't've been termed an infirmary, it should've instead been called 'Marist College Ashgrove's Multipurpose Boredom-Killing Centre.'

It goes without saying that you miss your family while you're at boarding school. Taking that into account, the infirmary helped to ease that burden. The infirmary was a place where you could go and talk, just talk, to a middle-aged woman. This kind of experience was unheard-of in a boarding school, for it seems middle-aged women tend to shy away from the splendours of all-boys boarding schools. But boarders needed that option, because it reminded us of talking to our mothers.

Other less significant things happened at or around the infirmary. Countless ambulances were called to the school because of skateboarding accidents or broken bones from rugby. Numerous times, kids have lined up for inoculations and vaccinations and injections. Thirty new boys' medical records enter the place every year, and probably very few records ever leave. But apart from the occasional interesting injury, the infirmary generally lay dormant.

The busiest time for the infirmary was when there were so many sick kids that they had to spill over into one of the dorms. I think at one time there were about thirty boys sick. That's a whole classroom full! If any more had been sick, scientists would've been called in to determine whether a new strand of the flu had spawned at our school. Anyway, thirty boys was the upward limit, and I think that's probably the fullest the infirmary ever was or will be.

What the infirmary did do was house the sick boarders at night time, so that they wouldn't interrupt the non-sick boarders' sleep. Boys also had the option of going to the infirmary during the night, if they felt ill. This was an experience to be avoided at all costs. However, in some cases, it was unavoidable. To illustrate this, an example must be drawn upon. The boy whose story I will use wishes to remain anonymous, so I will refer to him from now on as D. Tracey. No, wait, that's far too obvious. Daniel T. makes him much less identifiable...

Daniel had been sick all afternoon, and was trying desperately to get to sleep that Sunday night. The pain in his stomach got so bad that he decided it warranted a trip to the infirmary. On his way across the road from the year twelve dorm, he stooped, for this quelled some of the pain. But as he got halfway across, he was overcome with pain, and had to lie down in the middle of the road.. It was midnight, so there was very little, if any, chance of a car coming along, so he felt safe there.

After a few minutes, he got to his feet and made it the last few steps to the infirmary. He had a headache now, which complimented the pain in his stomach. He knocked on Brother Wayne's door, and waited for a reply. He heard the tinkering of a man who wasn't happy about being awake at the turn of the day. He waited while Brother got his keys, and opened the treatment room. After a salt gargle and two Panadol, Daniel was sent back to bed! But he followed Br Wayne's instructions.

A few hours later, he lay on his bed tossing and turning, until finally, at about a quarter past three, the pain was too much, and he headed back to the infirmary. Once there, Br Wayne was again unhappy about being reawoken. However, he realised that it must be a serious ailment, seeing as Daniel had returned. He once again took out his keys and opened the treatment room. This time he gave Daniel something stronger, before leading him to a bed in the infirmary. Daniel lay on the bed all night, and didn't get a wink of sleep.

The next morning, Daniel saw the doctor, and the doctor suspected appendicitis. Two hours later, Daniel was at hospital, and two days after that, he was still recovering in hospital – minus an appendix.

After his appendicectomy, the doctor who had operated on Daniel told him that he was in a life-threatening situation on the morning he had the operation. Lucky that Daniel had gotten to the infirmary the night before, because if he hadn't, then Br Wayne mightn't've taken him seriously, and he could've been sent back to class. Then the next day we would've all read in the paper:

SCHOOLBOY DIES OF APPENDICITIS AFTER SCHOOL NURSE REJECTION

That would've reflected very poorly on the professionalism of the nursing staff at MCA. And for the most part, the nursing staff in the infirmary are very professional.

Year Eleven

Year eleven was by far our most exciting year. We were situated in the grandest building on campus – the Tower Block. The Tower Block, or 'Tower,' as many people referred to it, was the first building erected at the site where Marist College Ashgrove now stands. It was a large, two-storey, U-shaped building, where three of the wings contained sleeping and studying areas, and the fourth contained three joint common rooms. Our cohort's time in the Tower Block was when we got into the most mischief. It was the time when we managed to get away with the most, and it was probably the time when we were hated the most by all of the staff.

To say that year eleven was a time for change would be an understatement. We had begun what was then known as our 'senior years' at school, and our exams were now counting toward our final exit mark. Stress was rampant toward the ends of the terms, and many no-hopers left.

Year eleven began as most years did, except for the fact that the dorm had been bombarded with new students. There were about twenty-five new students, and about thirty-five guys that had started at the school in year ten. It was a very uncomfortable time, those first weeks. Nobody knew who anybody was, and not even the veterans could steal a few minutes with each other to have a private discussion. However, we struggled on.

More than the usual number of new kids dropped out, mainly due to the fact that they were too old to be institutionalised. You see, it's hard to break new kids into the idea of boarding school – they just can't hack it. Too many of them are sent there because their parents can't or don't want to control them. They just end up having the same problems at boarding school as they did at home. They think they're top dog, but they're not at home any more, and their fellow boarders won't put up with as much crap as their mums are used to, so they are soon cut back down to size. Most of them don't like this, realise that they would be better off at home, and leave.

Pornography

Pornography is to boarding school what tax evasion is to the small business owner: naughty, enjoyable, and unavoidable. Having and/or watching pornography, or as it is more commonly known, 'porn,' is not only a rebellious act at boarding school, but a way of life! There is a reason why this chapter falls within the confines of year eleven; for although I was introduced to porn in the latter part of year nine, it was not until year eleven that the porn craze was so widespread. I believe the main reason for this sudden increase in concentration of pornographic material was the geometry of the Tower Block.

You see, the Tower was the ideal nesting ground for your average teenage porn addictee to carry out his most loved activity. There were about seventeen different areas that allowed the user the freedom to watch or read his material out of sight. In the rare case that a supervisor did enter the general vicinity of a person watching porn, the simplest option was to shut down Windows Media Player and bring up your English oral in the form of a Word document (or any other non-suspicious file).

Most of the porn present at boarding school was in CD form, simply because this was the most inconspicuous. However, at any one time, you can find porn of any medium at a boarding school.

Throughout my time at MCA, there were many major porn busts and raids. These occur when a supervisor thinks there is definitely too much porn present in the dorm, so he calls in all of the laptop computers in the dorm, and has the school computer expert, Mr Lee, check over them. The laptops stay in the custody of the supervisor until he is satisfied that all of the porn has been removed from the computers. At the same time this is happening, the supervisor will probably decide to search a few boys' areas for suspicious CDs. There was one particularly nasty porn raid that occurred in year ten. This raid yielded fifteen feature-length porn CDs. We made some quick calculations, and from our estimates, this was equal to about a third of the porn in the dorm.

Back in year nine, a mobile porn-burning shop was set up at the back of the middle dorm. This consisted of several laptops that were solely used for the watching and burning of porn. Whenever a supervisor did come down to the middle dorm (they rarely did), the students had plenty of time to either hide the computers or bring up inconspicuous documents.

The Birth of MSN

If the term isn't already in use, then I shall implement its use now: while I was at boarding school, we were living through the *technological revolution*. Things were changing, people were changing, and of course, education was changing to suit. One of the wonders that came with the constant waves of new technology was MSN: it was (and probably still is), an awesomely cheap way of socialising with friends who live a long way away. I won't bother to explain what MSN is, because if you don't know what it is, then you should probably skip this chapter (it will simply be too difficult for you to read).

MSN was celebrated amongst us boarders as our ticket to the outside world. It was something that we would do at home, as well as at school, and as such, it brought those two worlds closer together. We would sit for hours on the computers in the year eleven dorm conversing with chicks we hardly knew, and each other. Countless times, people would spend a whole day in there, just sitting and typing.

Theft

If there's one thing I would change about boarding schools, it would be theft. Theft is by far the worst thing that can happen in a boarding school

Boarding schools are filled with thieves. When parents send their children to boarding school, I think it's for one of two reasons: the first and most common reason is that they believe that their child/children will be better educated at the chosen school. The second, much more sinister reason is that the parents can no longer handle their kids because they're such little shits! It was always the shits that were the thieves at boarding school.

In year eleven, theft was particularly rampant. One specific night I can remember – it was towards the end of the year – about $2000 worth of gear went 'missing.' Our supervisors – in their mellow states – pleaded to the entire dorm to return the lost items. None of the items were returned. I remember this because it was so embarrassing the way our supervisors made it look like they were trying to get the stuff returned, when really they didn't even care. I was beginning to learn that this is a real problem we have in our society: people just don't care.

The supervisors I'm referring to will remain nameless – however, I will say that, although it isn't their fault those things were stolen, they certainly could've made a bigger effort in getting the things returned. It was a different case altogether when a supervisor's discman went missing…

It was Sunday morning, and all of us were preparing for a day in the city, away from the harsh realities of school life, when Mr Brunckhorst phoned the on-duty supervisor, saying that his discman had gone missing the night before, and to put a call over the loudspeaker so that people could keep an eye out for it. This was enough to get one of our dorm masters involved.

Either Mr Byrne or Mr Polzin got on the loudspeaker, and stated that no one was leaving until Mr Brunckhorst's discman was returned. This made me furious. Not only was this going to stop me from going out, it went against everything I believed in. This supervisor was going to punish the whole dorm because a staff member had lost his discman, and a week or two ago, he had not batted an eyelid when $2000 worth of stuff had gone missing! Naturally, I was enraged to hear later that Mr Brunckhorst had simply left his discman somewhere in his house.

Theft was present in every single dorm I lived in at boarding school. Not a week would go by without somebody having something stolen. I was one of the luckier victims, having probably $300 worth of stuff go missing in five years. But others had larger sums than this go missing in one hit. The most common thing stolen was money; next came mobile phones; and thirdly, pornography. These were the three things you had to keep a close eye on at all times.

Out of the ashes of theft rises some very humorous stories, one of which I will share with you now:

Con Beauchamp was one of the less hygienic members of the dorm. He was the one you avoided borrowing soap and shampoo from. Nevertheless, this didn't deter a certain somebody from stealing Con's toothbrush! Now for us, this was riotous! Firstly, why would somebody steal a toothbrush of all things? And secondly, if you were going to steal a toothbrush, why would you steal it from the smelliest, filthiest, most repulsive member of the dorm? It left us in no doubt that Con had simply lost his toothbrush.

The reason we discovered that Con's toothbrush had gone missing was that Con was constantly talking about it. The catchcry was, "Somebody's stolen my fucken' toothbrush." Even to this day, this line brings a smile to my face.

Fight Club

Fight Club. Now this was something that I will hopefully never witness again. The origins of Fight Club date way back to the year nine dorm. Fight Club was only small then, but it was so fun. Three quarters of the way through year eleven, Fight Club started up again – only this time, it wasn't so fun.

If you haven't seen the movie *Fight Club*, then I suggest you watch it before continuing this chapter.

I cannot recall exactly when in year eleven the idea of Fight Club was rehashed. What I can tell you is that it was the result of a great many coincidences: that we had the perfect dorm to conduct such an event, and at the same time, we had supervisors who were lenient enough to let it slide; that we had members of the dorm who didn't mind taking a beating, and other members who were ready and willing to dish out those beatings – and the list of coincidences goes on. But enough beating about the bush – let's get into the true nature of Fight Club.

Reg Reagan (from the footy show) once said that he didn't mind seeing two blokes go toe to toe. This was the essence of Fight Club: one man versus another – nothing else. Fight Club was held in an upstairs area of the tower, in the West Wing, as far away from the office as possible. Twenty or thirty people would cram into four boys' areas to witness two dorm members battle it out. Now, to many of you out there, this may seem like a very stupid and dangerous thing to do. But to many of us adolescent males, it was simply another form of entertainment, like computer games or TV.

There were very few rules to Fight Club. They included: no head shots, no crowd involvement, and when someone called 'bust,' Fight Club didn't exist.

Now I don't know how many matches were held while Fight Club survived, but I would hazard a guess at least twenty matches took place in year eleven. Many of the fights were weight class restricted (i.e. only certain people could fight each other – they had to be of similar weight). There were a few matches called 'bitch of the dorm' fights. These took place between two of the weaker members of the dorm, and these were the fights to watch, because unlike the heavyweights, the bitches couldn't hurt each other very much, and hence their fights tended to last longer.

As a general rule, the fights ended when one of the participants couldn't respond to their name, called 'stop,' or when one of the audience members called 'bust.' The first two reasons were for the safety of the fighters, and the last was for the safety of the audience; for although we thought we wouldn't get into much trouble, we didn't want to take any chances. When inevitably someone did call 'bust,' everyone ran. There was very little chance of anyone owning up to anything they did wrong at boarding school, unless they were confronted with it directly, and so it was in most people's best interest that the attitude of 'every man for himself' was employed.

We never got caught; however, a supervisor did once approach that area of the dorm between fights. So someone turned their music up really loud, and everyone started dancing! I don't know what the supervisor thought when he walked in to see twenty teenage boys dancing to Britney Spears' single 'I'm Not a Girl, Not Yet a Woman'!

In the end, he told us to tone it down, then left. One of three things could've been wrong with that supervisor that night; either he was too hungover from the night before to worry about disciplining us, or he thought he could gain our respect by letting us get away with something, or the third and most likely reason: he just didn't think there was anything wrong with a large group of testosterone-charged boys dancing together to a song which was most certainly targeted at a female audience!

The physical injuries sustained from Fight Club were too numerous for each to get a mention, so I will take stock of only the worst. Firstly, there was a broken arm; nothing too abnormal there, except when you take into account that the broken arm was sustained in a Fight Club match, blamed on a bad fall down some stairs, then the story was believed by not only the school nurse, but the boy's parents as well! If you asked me, I'd tell you this could be classified as negligence.

The second major injury was a split forehead. This occurred after a contestant was upset with his performance in the ring, moved promptly to the bathroom, where he headbutted a window 'Jackie Chan' style in frustration – broke the window, and then blamed the broken window on a stray football. Oh, you can blame just about anything on a stray football at a rugby-mad school and expect to get away with it.

The third and most gruesome injury was one of the beatings that a boy received. It was by far the worst injury I have ever seen as a result of a pre-arranged fight. This boy was comparable to a mouldy sun-dried tomato after his fight, his torso and upper arms were covered in bruises. This particular fight was the result of a smaller white boy foolishly challenging a larger black man-child.

In the end, there were no exceptionally grotesque disfigurements resulting from Fight Club. So at least in that respect we were mature. While many people would regard Fight Club as some teenage fun, I put it to you that it was a remarkably brainless exercise that we involved ourselves in. And if I had my time again, I would most certainly not involve myself in Fight Club. In saying that, however, I am forgetting how fun Fight Club actually was, and instead looking at it from a far more mature approach. So I will leave it up to you to decide how ludicrous this episode in boarding history appears.

Physics – No Worries

When we started school in year eight, the teachers took a lot of time to explain to us what plagiarism was. This hit us pretty hard. I mean we were only young, and already they were telling us that people our age were committing crimes. Although it is true that none of us really thought that the teacher was referring to us. It was *other people* who would plagiarise, and it was *other people* who would get caught.

Over the years, we learnt that it wasn't an easy task for a teacher to catch someone who had plagiarised; this gave rise to its growth. With widespread use of the internet for research, it was possible to gather an unlimited amount of information in seconds, and just as easy to copy it. It started in religion classes mostly. RE assignments would pass from person to person without so much as the batting of an eye. Nobody felt guilty when committing this apparently heinous act. People simply assumed that the original person who had written the assignment probably just cut and pasted it from the net, and so you were only plagiarising what someone had already plagiarised earlier.

There was however the rare occasion when people were caught. This usually occurred when large groups were involved...

We were heading into our first real exam block. The first semester exams had merely been practice for these. I was beginning to get stressed out, and I wasn't alone. People were just now realising that you have to study to get good grades in year eleven, you can't just wing it. The pressure was on, and everyone could feel it.

This exam block was especially bad, because it coincided with the due date for ten physics practical reports. On their own, the reports weren't that difficult, but when you had ten to do over a weekend, as well as five exams the next week – now that's when it becomes difficult.

Some boys seemed to be taking the stress fairly well. They were getting enough sleep, and didn't seem to be at everyone's throat all the time. But me, I was a wreck. I was like an adolescent female elephant with period pain and a mouth ulcer.

There were about ten boarders who studied physics, and all of them managed to hand their prac reports in on time. Some of the boys had been well prepared and had the pracs finished for a week; others had the liberty of a few days; however, some boys (and I was one of them) had to pull an all-nighter to make sure that all the pracs were finished on time.

A friend and I had decided that we would only write up every second prac, and then we would take each other's work and write up our own version, using the other as a base. It seemed like a pretty good idea at the time, but we probably left it a little late in the end. That is, if you call 3:00am 'late.' However, we were in a better position than some, who didn't get any sleep that night.

About two days after we'd all handed in our pracs, rumours started floating around. They were of the ilk that omitted names, but told the whole story. Apparently some boys had been caught plagiarising their physics pracs, and as a result were going to receive no credit for them. Now this was really big news. No one had been caught for plagiarism on a scale like this ever. The boys who did this were certainly not going to be happy.

When I first heard the rumour, I knew who the culprits were. The only reason they were caught was because they did it on such a large scale. There were four of them, and each of their pracs were almost identical! How could they expect to get away with it? I was of course sympathetic to their plea, because I hadn't been completely honest when I'd signed the authenticating statement on the bottom of my pracs either.

Tunnelling

Slowly but surely, our behaviour in year eleven worsened. We'd realised that we really couldn't get into trouble for anything, and so, we became very, very daring.

About three quarters of the way through year eleven, we were told that the Tower wasn't going to be used as a boarding facility after our year had gone through. The reason the headmaster gave us was that it was too expensive to bring the building up to standard as far as fire regulations go. Naturally, we felt fairly special being the last group to go through the Tower. However, at the same time, we realised that this was our chance to destroy as much of the Tower as we wanted, because the building was to be refurbished and transformed into offices. For future reference, it is not a good idea to tell teenage boys that the building they're staying in is up for renovation.

Basically, the headmaster had just prompted a free-for-all for the wannabe vandals in the year group. By the end of the year, there were broken windows and cupboard doors; there were smashed tiles, and cracked door frames; but by far the most prolific thing was the number of names written on the walls, desks, shelves and presses.

I don't know what the connection with graffiti and name writing, but the bond seems unbreakable. I would even go so far as to say that the most common form of vandalism is the perpetrator writing their own name somewhere. I can remember when two particular boys from the year eleven dorm must've had a concentrated outburst of vandalmania, because one day we all realised that their names were everywhere! Both of their names were written at least four times in my area alone! Most boys found themselves in my position, with about four tags in their area, so, on average this means that they must've written their names about three hundred times all over the dorm! The truth is, I felt genuinely jealous that I hadn't thought of the idea first. But I had to swallow my jealousy in order to seem uncondoning of the action.

Anyway, as the year drew to a close, workmen started floating into the dorm at different times, doing odd jobs, or taking measurements, and it was at this time that we made the greatest discovery about the Tower to date.

Earlier in the year, we had explored the attic of the Tower. It was disappointingly bare, not containing any old radios or diaries or anything (the Tower was used as an outpost during WWII). So we came down unfulfilled. However, the next thing that we exposed lead us to the other extreme.

The cleaner's closet generally remained shut, but not locked, during the term. On the rare occasion that you did look in there, you were merely overwhelmed at the school's stockpile of disposable towels, or marvelled at what ten litres of toilet disinfectant looks like. But towards the end of the year, all of the cleaning supplies were cleared out, and to our delight, there was a manhole, right in the middle of the closet! Trouble was to follow directly…

One, two, three… I had counted twelve people who had begun their expedition into the never-never. They were going to a place where no boarder had gone before, hopefully to a land of plenty, where boys and girls can live together, and not be separated by the harsh decisions of our parents. But no – in all seriousness, these boys were really only going to the other side of the dorm.

People had seen the hole, and that night there was no study to do (even though we were in exam block!) So a troop had outfitted itself with a torch and proceeded to climb into the hole, not to be seen again until fifteen minutes later.

They had allotted duties to some people who were destined to stay above ground. One was a lookout. They were patrolling, making sure that no supervisor would catch the boys who were tunnelling, whilst

ALL I LEARNED AT BOARDING SCHOOL

trying not to look too conspicuous. However, this was to no avail. When the boys were returning to the manhole, Mr Brunckhorst (or Mr No-Trouble) noticed a noise beneath his feet that seemed to be coming from inside the floor itself. On closer inspection, there was definitely a noise, but what was it? Then it hit him. He stamped the floor, and then summoned the boys up from under the floor.

Year Twelve

Is it all worth it? This is the most common question every year twelve student faces. Is the amount of time I put into study worth it, considering the results I will get? I asked this question of myself countless times throughout my schooling career, and especially in year twelve. I always came back with the same answer – yes. For although at times the going got tough, I could almost always see through to the light at the end of the tunnel.

For me, that was always a simple exercise. However I did sometimes wonder – what if I was a low achiever? What if I never got a break? What if things just never went my way? What you need at times to combat this entourage of questions is someone to put it into perspective for you.

Matthew Hayden came to our school toward the middle of term three of year twelve. I will never forget the stirring speech he made. He had three main points:

1. To always give everything your very best, to put absolutely everything into whatever you are attempting and to work your guts out to achieve the best possible result.

2. To always remember your parents – the ones who scraped for every penny to put you through school.

3. Finally, if all else fails, come back to Christianity.

That speech made a big impression on me and, I dare say, a lot of my peers. Many of us held the belief that Matthew Hayden didn't particularly like the school very much. But after that day – the day when he stood up at the lectern and began to cry as he perused over his time at MCA – we all knew that Matthew Hayden loved our school just as much as we did.

I was amazed to see such a cultural and sporting icon have a human moment. I'm not saying that Australia's sporting heroes aren't human, but ask yourself this question; how often do you see the Susie O'Neils, the Patrick Johnsons and the Elton Flatleys shed a tear when questioned about their schooling? I would expect the answers to range between 'not very often' and 'never'. The point I'm trying to make is that superstars are just normal people who are particularly good at what they do. They don't have X-Ray vision, and they can't jump over buildings in a single bound. They come from the planet Earth, and they need to be nurtured just like the rest of us.

Lingo

There were times at school when the language that the boarders used must've been so foreign to everyone else at the school. The main reason for this was that about a quarter of the boarders were from Papua New Guinea or the Solomon Islands, and English was their second language.

I've always wanted to know how to speak another language, and many of the boys I lived with had this gift!

Margaret Keetles

Mrs Keetles is a one-of-a-kind woman. In her own way, she is what I would describe as a power-woman; she is authoritative, influential, fair, and incredibly well spoken. She grabs your attention in a unique way, and this is only matched by her incredible ability to hold your attention while you are listening to some oration that is comparable to dog drool. You see, she was the person at our school that had the thankless task of continually reminding the year twelve cohort about QTAC, University, the QSA, the QCS test and other such things that we had to hear about, but didn't much care for.

In the end, however, she did a fine job of getting across her message to the students, though there were times when many of us wanted march right into the head office for the QSA and raze it to the ground – for the simple fact that this might quell the river of information that Mrs Keetles was receiving, and that, unfortunately, had to be passed onto us.

(By the way, if you have not been through year twelve in Queensland yet, or recently, then you will have no idea what some of these terms mean. I suggest no wider reading, as the only place you will find yourself is in the palace of boredom, being bombarded with Enters, Scaling, and Rankings, as well as OPs, FPs, SAIs, WTs, SRIs, MC I & MC II, and ESLAWHNPPOTTATHOOTPTATTUTs*; along with all of the aforementioned acronyms.)

*Extra Stupid Long Acronyms Which Have No Particular Purpose Other Than To Annoy The Hell Out Of Those People That Are Trying To Understand Them

Mr Jones

Mr Gary Jones was our boarding master for year twelve. He was a most intriguing man, of modest build, with an ever-growing bald spot. His physical appearance didn't change much; in fact, nothing about Mr Jones ever did change. He was the most peculiar man that I met during my schooling at MCA. Every year eighter was equipped with a fear of Mr Jones within their first term. He was the man who yelled at people, just metres from the chapel door, for talking during singing practice. He was the man who confiscated footballs for years at a time. He was the man whose office you were sent to if you did something extra bad. In short, he was the policeman of MCA.

Before year twelve, I had occasion to talk to Mr Jones only once, and that was in year nine. Webby and I were play-fighting out the front of the junior dining room when he walked along. As soon as we noticed him, we ceased our playful actions and took on a more solemn appearance; but Mr Jones had already seen too much. He yelled at us there and then, telling us not to muck around. I never admitted it, but when his face was inches from mine, and I could count his fillings, I was the most scared that I had ever been.

I don't think I will ever fully understand the way that Mr Jones operates. However, throughout year twelve, I became accustomed to how he worked. He had everything that he needed to say over the loudspeaker down pat. One of the commonest of his things to say was, '*It being twenty-five after seven, move over to the dining room for breakfast.*' He said this in his constant, unwavering stern voice, with emphasis on the words *it*, and *being*.

Mr Jones' wardrobe contained two kinds of outfits: suits (complete with cufflinks), or jeans, shirt, and sweater – nothing else. Mr Jones' suits were of the finest nature, and unlike other teachers, who often went with the open-collar look, he always wore a tie. Mr Jones' suits helped to create his identity. Something which he would know a lot about, considering his position in the day-school.

Mr Jones was not only the year twelve boarding master, but also the head of English in the day-school. On top of all this, he was a very heavy smoker – when did he find time for himself? I will never know how hectic Mr Jones' school days would have been, and for that I am grateful. I can only imagine how many people would've wanted a piece of his time, and it was his duty to oblige them. He was one of MCA's workhorses, even though he probably wouldn't care to admit it.

Mr Jones was very particular. When we were juniors, sometimes we would have our English work cross-marked by him. We would marvel at our work, as it came back scrawled over in green pen. You see, Mr Jones would only ever write in green pen – and not a ballpoint pen either, it had to be a green *ink* pen. I completely understand his reasoning for this now, but back then, it baffled me why someone would insist on writing in a pen colour which is so unorthodox. The reason was simple: it was so that he would know when something had been written by him. Think about it, how many people do you know that regularly write in green ink pens?

Another very strange thing that I noticed about Mr Jones was that he never carried things in his pockets. He always used to carry four things with him, and always in his hands: a green pen (of course), a packet of Dunhill cigarettes, his mobile phone, and his master key. I once asked him why he was the only person in the school in possession of a master key. He must've been in a bad mood that day, because he took it rather harshly – as if I was questioning his authority. But when he'd said his spiel once, about how he deserved much more than a master key, I didn't mention it again.

Year Eight Punishment

While I was in year twelve, the trend was for the junior dorm masters to send their worst-behaved kids for a stint in the senior dorm. I really do not know how this managed to stop the bad behaviour of the kids in trouble – but somehow it did. I do however know that if I was in year eight, I would've been paralysed in fear had I been sent to live in the year twelve dorm…

Boarding school has a way of ministering a certain poetic justice – this is one fine example of it:

Reece was the most recent ring-in from year eight to spend some time in the year twelve dorm. Apparently he had sworn at some teachers in the day-school, among other things, to get sent there. Everyone was immediately aware of his presence. He studied with us, he ate with us, and he went to bed when we did. This kid was way out of his league.

The initiation was steady at first; people farted on his head, and ridiculed him in general. All this he took with a grain of salt. It wasn't until Viv and Floyd got onto him that he was really scared.

ALL I LEARNED AT BOARDING SCHOOL

Now Viv is a big guy. Firsts Rugby, AIC 1, as well as Queensland – in the gym at least six or seven times a week. So was Floyd, but to a lesser extent. It was this hugeness, coupled with the fact that they were both of Islander heritage, that made them VERY SCARY PEOPLE!

One night during quiet time, they cornered Reece and asked him whether he was racist – Reece mumbled 'No,' but he was already crapping his pants. Viv confronted Reece, saying, 'WHAT THE FUCK? What did you say?' He continued on, while Reece kept mumbling that he was sorry, even though he hadn't actually done anything wrong. Now of course, both Viv and Floyd are actually quite nice blokes when you know them, and they were simply putting on an act to scare this poor defenceless year eighter.

Anyway, Viv and Floyd continued on like this for a while, telling Reece that they would come to him in the night, and do things to him that are far too disgraceful to print. The whole ordeal reminds me of jailbreak movies, and the scene where the little white guy has to take it like a bitch from a huge black guy. That black guy is usually called Bubba, and has a long-standing tradition of having his way with whomsoever happens to be his roommate.

Keith

I am sorry to include such a gloomy chapter in this book; however, I owe it to Keith to include him in some significant way.

Keith Coombs was a member of the graduating class of 2004 at Marist College Ashgrove. He was a boarder, an excellent sportsman, a scholar, a friend, and finally, an icon in the dorm. Overall, Keith was a kid that any parent would be proud to call their own. He was destined for success.

In the fourth term of year twelve, Keith came back to school with a small but noticeable lump on the side of his neck. This was passed off by most people as 'probably a swollen gland,' or 'just a bit of infection' – which is fairly standard for a swollen neck. However, the reason lots of people didn't pay any attention to Keith's neck was because Drake Chow (another year twelve boarder) had come back to school with half of his face numb. This was because when he had returned home via plane, he'd had an ear infection. The flight had caused the infection to spread right into his head, and so now, he was on heavy medication to fight the infection, as well as anaesthetic for the left side of his face. Keith struggled on.

About a week later, Keith went to the infirmary (that lovely place), to get his neck diagnosed, and this is where it all went to shit. The staff at the infirmary noticed immediately that Keith's swollen neck was not just a simple illness. So Keith was sent to a specialist. After some scans and other tests, the doctors were certain that the lump on Keith's neck was some sort of cancer. Eventually the cancer was diagnosed exactly, and Keith was booked in for nine months of chemotherapy.

Before Keith, I had never known anyone who had cancer. I hadn't known anyone to spend more than a day or two in hospital. And no one in my family had died since I was born. About the only hospital experience I had was getting four teeth removed under general anaesthetic because I was too much of a pansy to get them out in the chair. I was what you would probably call a surgery virgin.

I must admit, my first reaction when I heard about Keith was denial. I was so much of a sceptic that my mind wouldn't let me believe what was the truth: Keith had cancer. I couldn't understand the reasoning behind a healthy young man being struck down by this kind of ailment. I work on the basis of cause and effect. You get cold, you get sick; you don't wash your hands, you get sick; you exercise without warming up, you get injured. But there was no cause for this, no overriding factor. Keith did not deserve to become ill. And that was it.

We all hear about the friend-of-a-friend who died of breast/lung/throat cancer. But that's exactly what they are – a friend of a friend. There is no direct link. But with Keith, there was a direct link. I had known Keith for five years. He and I were in competition for the least organised members of the dorm (although I did a much better job of hiding my disorganisation). I knew that Keith enjoyed a good porno, and that once he'd seen one, he couldn't stop! I knew that Keith's modesty was his overriding emotion. I knew that Keith's favourite sleeping position in summer was on his stomach with his arms wrapped around a pillow nestled under his head. I knew so much about him that it didn't seem possible that it was *him* who was sick.

Nevertheless, I eventually came to believe that Keith was sick.

The Formal

According to the Macquarie Dictionary, the prefix 'over' is used to convey a sense of 'over the limit,' or 'in excess.' In schoolboy language, the use of the word 'rated' is quite excessive; the word has now taken on another meaning, is similar to the words 'like' and 'enjoy.' For example, instead of a group of teenage boys walking past a good-looking girl, and saying 'I like the look of her,' they would instead say, 'I rate her.' Pulling these two terms out of their separate places in our language, and placing them side by side, we come up with a new expression – *overrated*. And if there was one thing at boarding school that was overrated, it was the year twelve formal.

The formal occurred at the very end of term three. It was strategically placed at the end of our most important exams. Most boys would've spent weeks thinking about the formal, and the after-parties that went with it. The average price tag associated with preparations for the formal was around $500, but some boys went the whole hog, spending as much as

$2000 on a suit, and paying for the tickets, as well as cufflinks, corsages, and limo hire.

After collecting my date, and my aunty and uncle who were taking the place of my parents in the photos, we milled in the gym for about a decade waiting in line for our photographer to be ready. After that, it was time to head to the Sheraton where we would have our meals. My aunt and uncle dropped us off, and we headed inside. After an ordinary buffet, and some even worse dancing, it was time for the night to come to an end. I said goodbye to my partner, and headed to the post – never to see or hear from her again.

The post-party was infinitely better than the formal. Thirty deprived adolescent males, a dozen chicks, $1000 worth of alcohol, and nothing but the night (and early morning) to party into. Most people started out pretty hard, sculling their first beers; these were the boys who later in the night had a hard time keeping the buffet down. Drinking games were played, and a few boys got some action, but apart from that, it was just good for us to let our hair down for a while.

It certainly wasn't the best night of my school life, but it was the best night of that week. The thing that annoys me about the formal is the cost. To some people, $500 might be the change they keep in the ash tray; but to me and my parents, it was too much to spend. If only they could find a way of making the formal affordable for all. We certainly don't need cufflinks, they really overinflate the price.

Even the use of the word 'formal' as the title for this event is, I believe, a gross exaggeration. *'Formal': of or concerned with (outward) form or appearance; in accordance with rules, convention or ceremony; precise or symmetrical.* Of these three common definitions, our school formal adheres to only one. There were very few rules at the formal; for instance, at any one time, a plethora of boys were present in the toilets smoking. Also, although many people cared what they looked like at the commencement of the formal, by the time the night was drawing to a close, the year twelve cohort and our dates looked more like an out of control B&S rather than a high school formal. The only definition which seems to stick to our formal is the third definition. For although many weird and wonderful things happened on the night, nobody lost any body parts, and thus we were all just as symmetrical the next day!

Graduation

MCA's school song is the 'Sub Tuum.' While I was at school there, I probably sang that song about a thousand times. Something which I associate with that song nowadays is raw emotion – whenever I sang that song, there was always an emotion present: elation when we scored the winning try in rugby, solemnity in the chapel, grief in our slow return to school from Chandler – and the list goes on. However out of all those times that I sang 'Sub Tuum' at school, one rises above the rest when I take into account raw emotion. It was the final time that I sang the song in school uniform, it was the final time that I sang the song at the school, but most of all, it was the final time that I sang the song with all of my friends.

The graduation didn't technically start until Friday morning, but we had the awards night on the Thursday night. This consisted of the whole school, as well as any parents, family or friends who wanted to come, sitting in the gym for three hours while the academic awards for the year are handed out. Mostly it's meant for the year twelves I think, because their awards are personalised, whereas all of the non-senior awards are pretty standard.

The night was compulsory to attend, however, there was no roll taken, and I'm sure that many students gladly boycotted. However, being boarders (the heart of the school), and knowing the event was listed on the college's conditions of enrolment, we braved the three-hour ceremony as well as we could. I know that at the best of times it was boring for the students; I can't begin to comprehend what it must've been like for the parents and family members who attended. I mean, at least we knew a few of the people who were walking up on the stage as their names were called. The parents and friends would've been lucky if they knew half a dozen kids out of about 400 who were awarded! They would be entertained for about 1% of the entire evening.

In my time at school, I attended five awards nights. Most years, no one from my family was there, but they made up for it in the last year, when fifteen of my family were present to watch me collect my award for conspicuous effort in study. Going back to percentages, that was well over 1% of the people in attendance that night. If every student had been in attendance that night, and if every student had brought with them fifteen family members, then there would've been over 24,000 people present. Can you imagine fitting 24,000 people into the space of three basketball courts? I'd rather be a sardine!

After the awards night, our parents and families left us to spend our last night ever at boarding school. I cannot mention what happens on a night such as this for fear of prosecution; however, I will go so far as to say that I don't know anyone who didn't enjoy the night.

The next day we rose at about 7:30, and hopped straight back into our school uniforms which we had only shed less than twelve hours ago, and which we would stay in for the majority of the rest of that day. We made our way over to have our final breakfast at the college, but most people opted for a light meal, as the day was sure to bring fluctuating emotions, and the last thing we wanted was to be held down by a full stomach.

We all hung around the dorm until our parents arrived, and when they did, we slowly drifted up toward the gym. That morning we were to have the Graduation Mass, followed by the farewell for the seniors. My mum arrived, and I sent her up to the gym. The seniors amassed outside the gym at about a quarter to nine, just in time for everyone to be seated. Mr Robertson's address was very casual as he told us how we were to enter the gym, and then sit in the front four blocks. Looking back, I was amazed at how we all did exactly as we were told one final time. We lined up in two huge clusters, and snaked our way into the gym. Like sand through a funnel, we found our seats, and joined in the singing as best we could, for this would be our final hoorah, and our final blessing.

Schoolies

$5,000,000 worth of alcohol, 50,000 schoolies, 10,000 toolies, 200 high-rises, $95 worth of locksmith, 44 empty cans of midstrength, 36 reports of theft via flying fox, twenty more people in your room than what there's supposed to be, 17 randoms who think they know you, 3 death metal bands, and one very crowded avenue.

Schoolies was a time of discovery: self-discovery, group discovery, and of course, for us oh-so-sheltered boarders, a time of sexual awakening.

Schoolies started long before the final day of grade twelve for most people. I'd heard that some people had been organising schoolies since they were in year eleven – that's over a year of preparation for just one week. I speak from experience when I say that you don't need to start organising it that early – it's just a waste of time. For me, the schoolies experience started when my friends and I thought that we had better start organising something, or we might be too late to book any accommodation. So we grumbled, and groaned, and did some pottering around on the net, but none of us were really any good at organising those sorts of things. So the time came when someone told Mr X about a group of guys who had hotshot accommodation, and a few vacant spots left. Mr X then told Mr J, who alerted me, and thankfully all my friends and I managed to snap up the leftover possies before Mr Q heard about it. Because sure as eggs, Mr Q would've told Mr K, who would've blurted it to Mr H, and because Mr H didn't have any accommodation, he would've wanted to go, and then one of us might've missed out. I don't know why, but sometimes boarding school reminds me of a soapie.

So we had our spots, and for the moment, we were happy. But then came the deposits, and the photos, and the threats from the organisers about getting everything on time.

Fire engines are quite an unusual vehicle. Usually when you see them, you tend to wonder where the fire is. However, during schoolies, we came to recognise that fire engines are not always travelling to a fire, and that sometimes (in this case, usually) they are travelling to a false alarm. Each morning we would rise, sometimes after 11am, and without fail, each morning a fire engine would come sailing down the Gold Coast Highway, off to fight another set of invisible flames which had engulfed an accommodation building full of pothead schoolies – or so it seemed.

That was about the extent of our routine at schoolies. Otherwise, our week was just about as unorganised as possible.

Pregnancy – What the…?

I knew life would change once I left school. But I didn't think that it would change so suddenly, and with such momentous events! It all began on the Friday night of schoolies week. I was to referee at a touch football carnival planned for the weekend, so I decided to return to Brisbane for the night. One of my teachers, the undeniably selfless Ben Webb, had offered to transport me to and from the touch grounds while I stayed at his place. (The reason I couldn't stay with him on Friday night was because the teachers were having post-school drinks – it was the last day of school!) So I stayed at school on Friday night, and went to touch with Webby on Saturday morning as planned.

I refereed all day, getting more and more tired with each breath. Eventually I rang Webby and told him that I would be ready to be picked up at 6:30 pm (that was the conclusion of my last game), and he seemed fine with that.

So I finished my last game, running on heart rather than stamina, and then returned to the referee's tent. I plonked myself down on a white plastic chair, and tried to let the tension drain from my muscles. Then suddenly, there was this older couple standing in front of me, and the woman was asking me whether I was Daly Kelly. Now my immediate reaction when I saw them was to think that they weren't quite old enough to be grandparents – not yet. Little did I know how much truth this thought held. Anyway, I stood up, and we introduced ourselves, and apparently they were Ben's parents?! They went on to say that Kelly (Ben's wife) was pregnant (this I already knew), and that she was in labour!

I didn't understand, because they said it so calmly, but labour is a big thing! I wasn't really surprised until we got to Ben and Kelly's house, and I realised that she wasn't at the hospital, she was in the house, *in labour*! I thought to myself, *Why isn't she in a hospital?* On the inside I was a wreck – I was physically exhausted from the day. And now my mind had to try and deal with an experience unlike any other I had had before. I was freaking out. However, I didn't wish to stress out Ben or Kelly, who both looked tired and worn out themselves, so I tried to remain calm for their sake. Kelly – God bless her – was more worried about what I was going to have for tea, than for her child which was so obviously ready to be born.

I might never know just how Ben or Kelly felt that night. But I do know one thing: I was certainly not mature enough to successfully handle that sort of situation.

About the Author

Daly Kelly is a married man with five kids. He lives in Darwin where it's hot. He's an engineer and enthusiastic CrossFitter. He especially likes Flame Trees restaurant in Denmark, WA.

Appendices

All boarders who attended MCA as a member of the Graduating Class 2004:

Abraham Eke – Aba
Alfred Clay
Andrew Power – Powers
Andrew Schroter
Ashley Merlow – Magic
Brendan Corfield
Brenton Stone – Stony
Chris Sheehan – Sheeyak
Chrishan Zerner – Bubba
Colby List
Daly Kelly
Dan O'Connell
Daniel Humphries
Daniel Tracey
Donald Mawn
Douglas Laimo
Drake Chow – Rakishi/Ivan
Eric Bekefi
Eugene Shulze – Oigen
Floyd Dausabea
Glen Timo

Gregory Lock

Hamish Campbell – Hampbell

Harry Rueben

Joe Klekar

Joel Nicholls – Juga

Joey Buckerfield

John Crawley

John Fegan – Prongo

John-Bruce Mohr – JB

Joseph Walsh

Josh O'Connor

Julian McGruther

Keith Coombs

Kevin Patterson – Pato

Luke Phillot – Curly

Marco Zande

Mark (Akarachi) Wungwongpaiboon – Stiffy

Mark Kinsella

Matt Ferndale

Matthew Grew – Grewsa

Michael Kerwin – Kerpie

Michael Tilley

Morgan Midgely – Tripod

Neville Lai

Nicholas Huth

Peter Neeskens

Phillip Naden – Kiwi
Robert Lord – Bob
Sijmen Schippers
Stephen Hopkins – Hoppy
Stephen McPherson – Stevie Mac
Terry Laore
Thomas Kenny – Kendo
Viv Kelesi – Franke

How to Play Oxen:

Number of players: 4 or 6

Equipment required:
>1 set of standard playing cards (52)
>1 table; 1 chair for each player

Set Up:
>Each player receives four cards.

Idea of the Game:

The idea of Oxen is to get four of a kind, and then to have your partner call Oxen on you.

Start of Play:

The play starts when the dealer throws four cards down on the table face up – these are the communal cards.

Continuing Play:

You then exchange any of your cards for the cards that are available on the table. You cannot hold more than four cards in your hand. (this can continue for several minutes as the cards discarded by others may be of interest to you and vice versa – this usually starts as a quaint exchange and quickly moves to an aggressive manoeuvre!).

Once the communal cards are no longer of interest to anybody, the dealer can suggest that they are scrapped, and if everyone agrees, then those four cards are piled together, and placed in the discard pile. The dealer then takes another 4 cards from the deck and puts them face up on the table, and another round of exchanges occurs.

Calling Oxen:

At any point during the game if a player calls Oxen on another player then that is the end of that hand. If the targeted player has 4 of a kind in their hand, then one point is taken by the caller's team. If the player does not have 4 of a kind, then one point is taken by the targeted team.

You can play to 5 or 10 points (or however you see fit).

Sub Tuum

Sub Tuum Praesedium
Confugimus Confugimus
Sancta Dei Genitrix
Sancta Dei Genitrix

Nostras Deprecationes
Ne Despicias
Ne Despicias
In Necesitatibus Nostris

Sed a Periculus Cunctus
Libera No Semper
Virgo Gloriosa
Et Benedicta

Sub Tuum Praesedium
Confugimus Confugimus
Sancta Dei Genitrix
Sancta Dei Genitrix

www.ingramcontent.com/pod-product-compliance
Lightning Source LLC
Chambersburg PA
CBHW031257290426
44109CB00012B/623